Italian Takeout

Recipes

*Making Pizza and Pasta at Home is a Pleasure with
These Simple Italian Recipes!
(2022 Cookbook for Beginners)*

Ferro Alfonsi

CONTENTS

Introduction 5
History 6
Ingredients 7
Instruments and 9
Equipment
Methods of 10
Cooking

APPETIZERS
Sticks of 11
Mozzarella
Rice Balls 12
Deep-Fried
Parmesan 13
Eggplant
Bruschetta 15
Antipasto Misto 17
Italiano
Homemade 19
toasted ravioli

SOUPS
Minestrone 21
Pasta with Beans 23

RICES
Risotto with 25
Creamy
Mushrooms

SALADS
Caesar Salad 27
Salad Verde 29
Italiano
Caprese Salad 30
Salad with 31
antipasto
Gorgonzola with 32
pears

SANDWICHES
AND BREAD
Garlic Bread 34
Garlic Knots 35
Italian Sandwich 37
Vegetables 38
Grilled Panini
Hero Meatball 40
Parmigiana

PASTA
Pasta Made 41
From Scratch
Dough yields
Pasta Sauce from 43
Scratch
(Marinara)
Gnocchi 44
Bolognese 46
Meatballs on 49
Spaghetti
Alfredo 51
Fettuccine
Traditional 53
Lasagna
Creamy Pesto 54
Linguini
Carbonara 57
Fettuccini
Linguini al Frutti 58
di Mare
Spicy Shrimp in 60
a Creamy Sauce
Primavera 62
Puttanesca 63

PIZZA
Dough for Pizza 64
Pizza Sauce from 66
Scratch
Cheese pizza 68
Hawaiian Pizza 70
Super Meat 72
Pizza
Pizza with 74
Pepperoni
Pesto Veggie 75
Pizza
Pizza Bianca 77
Pizza with Spicy 79
Sausage and
Mushrooms
from Italy
Pizza with BBQ 81
Chicken

CHICKEN
Parmigiana 83
chicken

DESSERT
(DOLCI)
Tiramisu 86
Cannoli 88

Conclusion 90

Introduction

Italian cuisine is ingrained in American society. Pizza and pasta are Italian-American culinary classics. Though some may not consider Italian-American recipes to be genuine, they unquestionably represent the qualities that define Italian food — passion, freshness, palatability, and simplicity.

Food in Italy has always been regional, with each area having its specific taste or cooking style. Perhaps America has evolved into another "region" with its own particular Italian culinary style.

History

As with other immigrants, Italians who arrived in the United States as early as 1880 brought their unique cuisine with them. The bulk of the immigrants came from southern Italy, including Calabria, Abruzzi, and Sicily, and have left their stamp on Italian-American food.

These immigrants adapted to their new surroundings by using available materials to produce new cuisine. One example is spaghetti with meatballs. Whereas in Italy, meat was kept for rare occasions, the easy availability of ground beef gave rise to the meatball. It was drowned with marinara sauce, which quickly became the most popular sauce because to the widespread availability of canned tomatoes. The same scenario occurred with pasta, which was one of the few other Italian foodstuffs accessible in the US at the time.

Aside from immigration, troops returning from WWII were yearning for the Italian food they had enjoyed while stationed in Italy. This resulted in an increase in the number of enterprises opening to satisfy the needs of this new market.

From the humble pizza of Naples, which generally comprised of basil, garlic, and tomato, American pizza has grown, with tomato sauce and a variety of toppings.

American towns now have their own unique "Italian" foods, such as Philadelphia's Philly cheese steak, New Orleans' muffuletta sandwich, and chicken tetrazzini, as well as San Francisco's cioppino.

As various ingredients become more readily available, Americans are eagerly adopting traditional meals. Many new restaurants have opened, offering authentic Italian cuisine as well as fusion meals that combine Italian and other American tastes and ingredients.

Ingredients

The essential components of Italian cookery are considered to be olive oil, garlic, and herbs. These, together with the supplies mentioned below, will help you get started on your Italian culinary adventure.

Vinegar of Balsamic Origin (Aceto Balsamico)
A sweet-sour vinegar created in Italy from reduced and aged Trebbiano grape juice. Marinades, dips, sauces, and salad dressings are all made using it.

Fresh basil (Basilico) is preferred. Basil has come to be considered a plant that is uniquely Italian. Sweet basil is a herb that is widely used in sauces, salads, and soups.

Fava beans (Fagioli)
These are often used in soups, pasta dishes, and stews. Cannellini (white kidney beans), fava beans, and chickpeas are popular beans.

Cheddars (Formaggio)
Italian cheeses are very varied, with practically every area in Italy producing its unique kind. Pasta, sandwiches, pizza, and desserts all include cheese. Asiago, fontina, Gorgonzola, mascarpone, mozzarella, and Parmigiano-Reggiano (Parmesan cheese) are well-known cheeses.

The herb garlic (Aglio)
Garlic is often used in soups, stews, sauces, and grilled meats in Italy.

Medicinal plants (Odori)
Flavoring herbs such as oregano, sage, and thyme are often used in cooking.
For smashing vegetables and herbs, use a pestle and mortar.

Pasta
Thin sauces are thought to pair well with thin pasta, whereas richer sauces go well with tubular pasta. Spaghetti, lasagna, macaroni, fettuccine, rotini, linguine, penne, cannelloni, and rigatoni are some of the most well-known pastas.

Olive oil (Olio d'Oliva) is a common ingredient in Italian recipes. Distinct locations' oils have slightly different tastes. High-quality olive oil is considered to be extra-virgin, first-pressed, and cold-pressed. DOP, or 'denomination of origin,' signifies that it fulfills local government criteria. Chefs advocate using extra-virgin olive oil for salads and finishing, while ordinary olive oil may be used for lengthier or higher-temperature cooking.

Arborio or Carnaroli rice is used because it cooks to a creamy consistency, which is ideal in risotto.

Tomato (Pomodoro) Italian-American cuisines made more use of canned tomato, tomato sauce, and tomato paste, since they were more readily accessible to Italian immigrants in the past, while the identical dishes in Italy would have called for fresh tomato. This might be one of the most noticeable contrasts between Americanized Italian cuisine and real Italian foods.

Vino (Vino)
Wines, both red and white, are used to improve the taste of foods.
Marsala is a sweet wine that is used in recipes such as Chicken Marsala. It may be replaced with brandy, sherry, or port.

Instruments and Equipment

To create traditional Italian cuisine, all you need is a traditionally well-equipped kitchen. Some additional equipment may be required to prepare handmade pasta and pizza dough.

Grater for cheese
Choose one with at least two sides and a variety of grating sizes. Soft cheeses, such as mozzarella, need a bigger grating size, whilst tougher cheeses, such as Parmesan, demand a smaller grating size. A rotary grater is also excellent for shredding huge volumes of cheese.

Pressed Garlic
This is especially useful since Italian cookery necessitates the use of a lot of garlic. The garlic clove may be crushed by inserting it unpeeled into the press.

Knives
For chopping meat and vegetables, a variety of sizes will come in helpful.

If you want to create handmade pasta, a pasta maker is a must-have. Any chef can simply manufacture a variety of pastas using various attachments with this and an excellent pasta dough.

Drying Rack for Pasta
A rack with "arms" for hanging newly made pasta and keeping it in shape while drying.

Pizza Wheel vs. Pizza Cutter
To make it easier to cut cooked pizza, pastry, or uncooked dough.

Peel a pizza
A shovel-like instrument for securely and conveniently inserting or removing a hot pizza from an oven. It is often constructed of wood, however it may also be made of metal.

Pizza Stone A kind of pizza dough cooking surface composed of stone, ceramic, firebrick, or other materials. Although any baking sheet or tray will suffice, a pizza stone is touted to produce a better-tasting and more-textured pizza dough.

Draining Basket for Pot
To make it easier to cook pasta. After cooking, the pasta may be rapidly drained by pulling it out.

Spoons made of wood
Keep a variety of sizes on available for mixing sauces, batters, and other mixes.

Methods of Cooking

Italian cuisine is often fast and easy, with an emphasis on the quality and freshness of the ingredients. Boiling, steaming, sautéing, braising, frying, stewing, and grilling are all common cooking techniques.

Meat is braised by gently cooking it in a tight-lidded pot with vinegar, wine, water, broth, or tomatoes. This is done to tenderize and taste the meat.

Ingredients are sautéed in heated oil, and tastes are increased by reduction and caramelization. Deep-frying is done using grapeseed or other cooking oils rather than olive oil.

Allowing pasta to absorb flavor from the sauce makes it tastier.
This is accomplished by removing the pasta a minute before it is due to be done and cooking it for a minute or two in the sauce with a little of its cooking water. Because Italians want their pasta al dente or firm to the bite, they may cook it for a shorter period than specified on the package.

Now that you've stocked your kitchen with the essential materials and tools, it's time to try your hand at making some delectable Italian takeaway meals.

APPETIZERS

Sticks of Mozzarella

12 people
Time to Prepare: 10 minutes
Time to cook: 5 minutes

1 cup Italian style bread crumbs two
eggs
1 Tbsp. milk
1 pound mozzarella cheese, sliced
into 34-inch-by-34-inch strips
1 quart of vegetable oil
Topping: tomato sauce
Garnish with fresh basil

Directions
1. Whisk together the eggs and milk in a mixing basin.
2. Put the bread crumbs in a separate dish or on a tray.
3. Dip the cheese first in the egg mixture, then in the bread crumbs.
4. Coat the cheese evenly in the egg mixture and then in the bread
crumbs a second time.
5. Heat the oil in a skillet over medium heat.
6. Fry the cheese for 1 minute on each side, or until golden brown.
If you fried it for too long, the cheese will drip.
7. Pat dry with paper towels.
8. Garnish with finely chopped basil and serve with tomato sauce.

Rice Balls Deep-Fried (Arancini Di Riso)

4-6 people
Time to Prepare: 15 minutes
Time to cook: 15 minutes

Ingredients
1 cup seasoned bread crumbs
(Italian style)
2 cups cooled cooked risotto
½ cups of Italian style
seasoned bread crumbs
½ cup freshly grated Parmesan
¼ cup fresh basil leaves, finely chopped
 2 eggs, beaten 4 ounces
½ inch cubes of Gorgonzola Vegetable oil for frying

Directions
1. Place the bread crumbs in a medium mixing dish and set them aside.
2. Combine the risotto, bread crumbs, Parmesan, basil, and eggs in a mixing bowl.
3. Scoop out approximately 2 teaspoons of the risotto mixture at a time and roll into 14-inch balls. Dampen your hands to prevent the rice from sticking to them.
4. Place a Gorgonzola cube in each ball and close to cover the cheese.
5. Roll the balls in bread crumbs to coat.
6. Pour roughly 2-3 inches of oil into a heavy-bottomed skillet or pot.
7. Cook over medium heat for approximately 2 minutes, or until a cube of bread browns (350°F).
8. Fry the balls for 4 to 5 minutes, rotating periodically, until golden. Avoid overcrowding the pan.
9. Drain on paper towels before serving.

Parmesan Eggplant
(Parmigiana Di Melanzane)

Preparation Time: 20 minutes

Servings: 6
Time to cook: 45 minutes

Ingredients
2 peeled and cut into 1/2-inch slices eggplants

For the slices of eggplant
1 tbsp salt, or as desired, preferable kosher or sea salt
1 cup bread crumbs (Italian style)
1/4 cup Parmesan cheese, grated
2 beaten eggs

Layers of eggplant parmigiana
1 jar garlic-and-tomato pasta sauce (28 oz.) or homemade pasta sauce
1/4 cup Parmesan cheese, grated
4 cups or 16 ounces of shredded mozzarella cheese
 1/2 teaspoon dried basil

Directions

1. Season both sides of each eggplant slice well with salt. Place the eggplant slices in a colander and set aside for 1-3 hours to "sweat."
2. Wipe the eggplant slices dry using paper towels after they have sat for a few minutes.
3. Preheat the oven to 350°F and butter a baking sheet once the eggplant slices are ready.
4. Combine the bread crumbs and Parmesan in a mixing basin.
5. Coat the eggplant in the breadcrumb mixture after dipping it in the beaten eggs.
6. Arrange the pieces in a single layer on the baking sheet.
7. Bake until both sides are gently browned (approximately 6-10 minutes on each side).
8. Begin layering the sauce, eggplant, and cheeses.
9. Begin with a layer of spaghetti sauce in a 9x13 baking pan.
10. Add a layer of eggplant on top of that.
11. Top the eggplant with 1 tablespoon Parmesan and 1 to 1 13 cup shredded mozzarella.
12. Continue stacking, finishing with a cheese layer.
13 Bake until the cheese is golden brown, approximately 15 minutes (about 35 minutes)

Toast with Garlic, Tomato, and Olive Oil (Bruschetta)

4-6 people
Time to Prepare: 10 minutes
Time to cook: 15 minutes

Ingredients
1 baguette, split in half lengthwise and gently toasted
¼ cup Parmesan cheese, grated
½ cup shredded mozzarella (optional)

As a garnish
2 tbsp. minced garlic (fresh or from a jar)
three tbsp extra-virgin olive oil
2 ½ cup coarsely chopped minced tomatoes
1/3 cup finely sliced fresh basil leaves
2 tbsp balsamic vinaigrette
½ teaspoon of salt
1 teaspoon black pepper, freshly ground

Directions

1. Mix together the topping ingredients and set them aside for 15 minutes to enable the flavors to emerge.
2. To serve, cut the toasted baguette into quarters.
3. Top with the tomato mixture and, if wanted, sprinkle with the cheeses.
4. Toast the bread to melt the cheese (about 5-10 minutes).

Platter of Appetizers (Antipasto Misto Italiano)

6 servings Preparation Time: 15 minutes
Time to cook: 0 minutes

Ingredients
3 cups torn, sliced, or cubed mozzarella cheese (or any cheese of preference, such as provolone or bocconcini)
20 slices of prosciutto (or other cold meats from Italy such as pancetta, pepperoni, salami, capicola, and so on)
3 (8 12 or 10 ounces) jars of olive oil-drained vegetables (olive, artichoke, tomato, giardiniera, mushroom, peppers, onions, etc.)
3 tbsp olives (mixed)
12 cup cherry tomatoes, halved Parmesan, shaved
1 loaf of sliced and toasted ciabatta bread
1 garlic clove, smashed into a paste

For basil-infused oil
1 cup fresh basil, trimmed
18 teaspoons of salt
3 tablespoons vegetable oil (reserved)

Directions

1. Arrange the ingredients on a big platter in tiny stacks. The goal is
to achieve a "rustic" appearance.
2. Garnish the cold slices with shaved Parmesan.
3. Crush the basil and salt into a pulp using a mortar and pestle.
Combine this with a little of the saved oil.
4. Drizzle the basil oil over the cheese and veggies.
If desired, drizzle extra olive oil over the plate.
5. Rub the garlic on the ciabatta bread and drizzle with olive oil
generously. Serve with this on top of the plate. Allow the meats to
come to room temperature before serving if they are cold.

Homemade toasted ravioli.

Serves : 6-8
Time to Prepare: 30 minutes
Time to cook: 20 minutes

1 (16 ounces) box beef ravioli, fresh or thawed
2 c. flour
¼ cup water 2 big eggs, beaten
2 cups bread crumbs (Italian)
1 tsp garlic powder
Deep-frying vegetable oil
For dipping, use marinara sauce.

Directions

1. Preheat a deep fryer to 350 degrees Fahrenheit.
2. In a mixing basin, combine the eggs and water.
3. Combine the bread crumbs and garlic salt in a separate bowl.
4. Coat the thawed ravioli in flour, then in the egg mixture, and last
in bread crumbs. If necessary, re-dip in the egg to coat evenly.
5. Arrange the coated ravioli on a piece of aluminum foil or on a
tray.

6. Fry the ravioli in batches until golden brown (approximately 1 minute).

7. Pat dry with paper towels and serve with marinara sauce.

SOUPS

Minestrone

8 servings
Time to Prepare: 0 minutes
Time to cook: 45 minutes

Ingredients:

3 tbsp olive oil
1 small onion, minced ½ stalk celery, minced 4 garlic cloves, minced
1 cup Italian chopped frozen green beans
½ cup diced zucchini
4 cups veggie broth
1 can of chopped tomatoes (14 oz.)
½ cup carrot, julienned 2 (15 ounces) cans red kidney beans,

drained 1 (15 ounces) can tiny white beans or great northern beans,
drained
3 cups boiling water
2 teaspoons minced fresh parsley
½ tsp oregano dried
1 ½ tsp powdered black pepper, or to taste
½ tsp dried basil ¼ tsp dry thyme
4 cups fresh baby spinach or cabbage, sliced
½ cups little shell pasta and ½ cups red wine

Directions

1. In a large saucepan, heat the olive oil over medium heat.
2. Saute the onion, celery, garlic, green beans, and zucchini in a skillet until the onions start to turn translucent (about 5 minutes).
3. Combine the vegetable broth, drained tomatoes, beans, carrot, hot water, and spices in a mixing bowl (parsley through thyme).
4. Bring the soup to a boil, then lower to low heat and continue to cook for 20 minutes.
5. Stir in the spinach or cabbage, pasta, and red wine.
6. Cook for approximately 20 minutes, or until the pasta reaches the appropriate consistency.

Pasta with Beans (Pasta e Fagioli)

6-8 people
Time to Prepare: 5 minutes
Time to cook: 30 minutes

Ingredients:
 1 tbsp olive oil
1 pound minced beef
1/4 cup pancetta, diced (optional)
1 small sliced onion
2 chopped tiny carrots
1 tiny chopped red bell pepper
1 can (28 oz.) chopped tomatoes, undrained
1 (16 oz.) can of drained white kidney beans
2 cups beef broth
1 1/2 teaspoon oregano
1 tsp pepper
 3 tsp parsley
1 jar (10 oz.) tomato sauce
1 cup ditalini or other pasta, cooked according to package directions
Parmesan cheese, grated

Directions

1. In a pan, heat the oil and brown the meat.
2. Cook until the pancetta (optional) is gently browned.
3. Saute the onion, carrots, and pepper until soft (about 5 minutes).
4. Drain the fat from the mixture and transfer it to a soup pot.
5. Bring the other ingredients, EXCEPT the pasta and Parmesan, to a boil. Reduce the heat to a gentle simmer.
6. Simmer, stirring periodically, until the veggies are soft and the soup has reached the desired consistency (8-10 minutes).
7. Stir in the cooked ditalini and heat through (approximately 1 minute).
8. Garnish with grated Parmesan before serving.

RICES

Risotto with Creamy Mushrooms

2 people
Time to Prepare: 5 minutes
Time to cook: 30-35 minutes

Ingredients
2 cups chicken broth
3 tablespoons unsalted butter, softened
½ small onion, chopped
½ cup Portobello mushrooms, sliced
¾ cup Arborio rice
¼ cup dry white wine
¼ cup Parmesan, finely grated
Salt and freshly-ground pepper, to taste

Directions

1. Heat the broth in a medium saucepan over medium heat.
2. Reduce the heat to low in order to keep the soup warm.
3. Melt 2 tablespoons butter in a medium saucepan over medium heat.
4. Cook the onion and mushrooms until they are soft (about 3 minutes).
Take out the mushrooms and put them aside.
5. Stir in the rice well.
6. Pour in the wine and continue to cook until it is nearly dry (about 1 minute).
7. Add half a cup of hot broth and simmer, stirring constantly, until the rice absorbs it (about 2 minutes). Repeat with a half-cup at a time.
8. Let the broth absorb completely before adding more. The rice should have a creamy texture, yet the grains should be supple but solid to the biting (about 20 minutes).
9. Remove from the fire and add the remaining butter, Parmesan cheese, salt, pepper, and mushrooms.

SALADS

Caesar Salad

Serves 6 people.
Time to Prepare: 10 minutes
Time to cook: 10 minutes

Ingredients
Caesar Salad Dressing
2 small cloves garlic, minced
1 teaspoon anchovy paste
Juice of 1 lemon
1 teaspoon Dijon mustard
1 teaspoon Worcestershire sauce
1 cup mayonnaise
½ cup freshly grated Parmigiano-Reggiano
¼ teaspoon salt
¼ teaspoon freshly ground black pepper

Croutons
2 tablespoons butter
2 tablespoons extra virgin olive oil
2 cloves garlic, halved
3 cups French or Italian bread, sliced into ½-inch cubes
Salt and pepper

For salad
½ cup Parmesan cheese, shredded, plus more for topping if desired
2 heads of romaine lettuce, torn into bite-sized pieces

Directions
To make the dressing
1. Combine the garlic, anchovy paste, lemon juice, Dijon mustard, and Worcestershire sauce in a mixing bowl.
2. Combine the mayonnaise, Parmigiano-Reggiano, salt, and pepper in a mixing bowl.
Combine thoroughly.
3. Taste and adjust the quantities as desired.
4. I will keep it in the refrigerator for 2 weeks.

To make the croutons
5. Preheat the oven to 350 degrees Fahrenheit.
6. In a saucepan over low heat, melt the butter, olive oil, and garlic.
7. Once the butter has melted, remove the pot from the heat.
Allow it to stand for 10 minutes before removing the garlic.
9. Add the bread cubes and toss to coat.
10. Arrange the bread cubes on a baking sheet and bake until golden brown (approximately 10 minutes), stirring the pan once or twice.
11. Remove the pan from the oven and place it on a cooling rack to cool.

To make the salad
12 Toss the lettuce and croutons in the dressing until well covered.
13. Add the Parmesan cheese and stir gently.
14. Garnish with more Parmesan, if preferred, and serve.

Salad Verde Italiano

Preparation: 4 Serves: 4 Refrigeration time: 2 hours
Time to cook: 0 minutes

Ingredients
For dressing
¼ cup white vinegar
2 tablespoons sugar
½ cup mayonnaise
2 cloves garlic
½ teaspoon Italian seasoning
½ teaspoon dried parsley
1 teaspoon olive oil
Juice half a lemon
¼ cup Parmesan cheese

For the salad
1 head lettuce, chopped
2 tomatoes, cut into wedges
½ can medium black olives
2 cups croutons
8 pepperoncini peppers
2 cups mozzarella cheese, shaved or torn into small pieces
½ teaspoon salt
1 teaspoon pepper

Instructions for the dressing
1. In a blender, combine all of the ingredients and mix until smooth.
2. Chill for at least 2 hours.

To make the salad
3. Toss all of the ingredients together.
4. Serve with the dressing on the side, or mix the salad with the dressing.

Salad Capri's Tomato and Mozzarella (Caprese Salad)

4-6 people
Time to Prepare: 45 minutes
Time to cook: 0 minutes

Ingredients
4 huge tomatoes,
1/4 inch thickly cut
1/4 cup packed fresh basil, rinsed and dried 1 pound fresh mozzarella, cut 14 inches thick
1/3 teaspoon crushed dry oregano
three tbsp extra-virgin olive oil
To taste, fine sea salt
To taste, freshly ground black pepper

Directions
1. Arrange the tomato and mozzarella slices on a serving plate in an alternating pattern.
2. Drizzle with olive oil and sprinkle with oregano.
3. Season with salt and pepper to taste.

Salad with antipasto

4 servings
Time to Prepare: 10 minutes
Time to cook: 0 minutes

Ingredients
8 cups romaine lettuce heart, chopped
¼ pound Genoa salami, diced
¼ pound pepperoni, diced
2 cups giardiniera (Italian pickled vegetables), coarsely chopped
12 pitted black olives, coarsely chopped
12 jumbo green olives, pitted, coarsely chopped
1 (8 ounces) jar of roasted red peppers, drained and diced
1 (6 ounces) jar marinated artichoke hearts, drained
¼ red onion, sliced into rings
2 tablespoons balsamic vinegar
¼ cup extra-virgin olive oil
1-2 tablespoons Italian Vinaigrette (optional)
Salt, to taste
Freshly ground pepper, to taste
½ cup Gorgonzola crumbled (optional

Directions

1. In a mixing dish, combine the first 9 ingredients (through red onion).
2. Season with salt and pepper before drizzling with olive oil, balsamic vinegar, and/or Italian vinaigrette (optional).
3. Gently toss everything together. If desired, garnish with crumbled cheese.

Gorgonzola with pears

Serves 2
Time to prepare: 15 minutes + 30 minutes sitting time
1 hour of cooking time

Ingredients
Italian Vinaigrette
⅓ cup white wine vinegar
¾ teaspoon dried oregano
½ teaspoon dry mustard
1 teaspoon salt
1 pinch of black pepper
⅛ cup red onion, finely chopped
1 ½ teaspoon garlic, minced
¾ cup olive oil

Spiced Walnuts

1 egg white
1 tablespoon water
2 cups walnuts, halves, and pieces
½ cup sugar

1 teaspoon cinnamon
½ teaspoon allspice

For the salad
1 red pear, cored and thinly sliced
3 cups mixed greens, washed and chopped
2 tablespoons Gorgonzola cheese, crumbled, plus more for garnish
½ cup spiced walnuts, chopped
¼ cup dried cranberries
½ cup Italian vinaigrette

For the spiced walnuts, follow these instructions.
1. Preheat the oven to 225°F. Line a shallow baking dish with foil.
2. In a mixing basin, whisk together the egg white and water until frothy.
3. Add the walnuts and toss to coat.
4. Using a strainer, drain them for 3 minutes.
5. Shake together the sugar, cinnamon, and allspice in a plastic bag.
6. Place the walnuts in the bag, close it, and shake to coat.
7. Arrange the nuts in a single layer on a baking sheet coated with foil.
8. Bake for 1 hour, stirring every 15 minutes, until golden brown.
9. Allow it to cool fully before storing it in an airtight container.
To make the vinaigrette
10. In a blender, combine all of the ingredients EXCEPT the olive oil.
11. Pulse a few times, then combine, adding a little olive oil at a time. Don't pour in the olive oil all at once.
12. Blend well and set aside for 30 minutes.
To make the salad
13. Prepare the pear and lettuce while the nuts bake and the vinaigrette sit.
14. When everything is done, toss the lettuce with the vinaigrette.
15. Toss in the remaining ingredients.
16. Garnish with more crumbled cheese before serving.

SANDWICHES AND BREAD

Garlic Bread

Serves 4-6 people.
Time to Prepare: 10 minutes
Time to cook: 30 minutes

Ingredients
2 teaspoons garlic, finely chopped
¼ teaspoon salt
¼ cup unsalted butter softened
1 tablespoon extra-virgin olive oil
2 tablespoons fresh flat-leaf parsley, finely chopped
1 loaf of Italian bread, about 15 inches long, 3-4 inches wide

Directions
1. Preheat the oven to 350 degrees Fahrenheit.
2. Mash the garlic with the salt in a mortar and pestle until it becomes a paste. Place it in a basin.
3. Pour in the butter and oil. Blend until smooth.
4. Add the parsley and mix well.
5. Cut the bread into 1 inch thick slices without cutting all the way through the bottom.
6. Sandwich the pieces together with garlic butter.
7. Wrap the bread in aluminum foil. Bread may be kept cold at this stage and then thawed to room temperature.
8. Bake for 15 minutes at 350°F.
9. Remove the foil and bake for another 5 minutes. As you serve, separate the slices.

Garlic Knots

Serves: 24
Preparation time: 45 minutes, plus 2 hours for proofreading.
Time to cook: 20 minutes

Ingredients
1 recipe Basic Pizza Dough
½ cup unsalted butter
3 tablespoons garlic, minced
1 tablespoon olive oil
1 teaspoon coarse sea salt
¼ cup grated Pecorino Romano or Parmesan cheese
2 tablespoons chopped fresh parsley

Directions
1. Make a batch of Basic Pizza Dough and let it rise.
2. In a small saucepan over low heat, cook the garlic in the butter until aromatic (about 3 minutes).
3. Cover the pot, take it from the heat, and put it away to keep warm.
4. Preheat the oven to 375°F and coat two large baking sheets with cooking spray.
Set things aside for now.
5. Turn the rising dough out onto a lightly floured board.
6. Roll out the dough using a floured rolling pin. Make a 16x12-inch rectangle out of it.
7. Drizzle olive oil over the dough.
8. Divide the dough in half lengthwise.
9. Cut the dough into 14-inch pieces crosswise.
10. Tie each strip loosely into a knot and set it on the prepared baking sheets, leaving a 2-inch gap between them.
Season the knots' tops with salt.
11. Cover with a towel and set aside for 30 minutes in a warm area.
12 Bake for 20 minutes, or until golden brown.

13. Meanwhile, combine the cheese and parsley with the heated butter mixture and well combine.

14. Dip the freshly cooked knots in the cheese-and-butter mixture and serve warm.

Italian Sandwich

Preparation Time: 10 minutes
 Servings: 2
Time to cook: 0 minutes

Ingredients
2 12-inch Italian style hoagie or sub rolls
¼ pound thinly sliced prosciutto or mortadella
¼ pound thinly sliced capicola
¼ pound thinly sliced provolone cheese
¼ pound thinly sliced Genoa salami
4-6 large lettuce leaves
1 thinly sliced large tomato
1 thinly sliced white onion
2 tablespoons olive oil, divided
4 teaspoons red wine vinegar, divided
Salt, pepper, Italian oregano
Pepperoni or fried sweet peppers (optional)

Directions
1. Cut each roll horizontally but not completely through.
2. Layer on 4 slices each of prosciutto, capicola, provolone cheese, and Genoa salami for each one.
3. Arrange lettuce, tomato, onion, 1 tablespoon oil, 2 tablespoons vinegar, salt, pepper, oregano, and pepperoni on top (optional).
4. Cut and serve

Vegetables Grilled Panini

Serves 4 people.
Time to Prepare: 15 minutes
Time to cook: 10 minutes

Ingredients
1 medium eggplant, sliced diagonally into ¼-inch strips
1 medium onion, peeled and sliced into ¼-inch rounds
1 red bell pepper, stem, and seeds removed, sliced into 8 pieces
1 medium yellow squash or zucchini, sliced into ¼-inch strips
½ cup canola oil, divided
Salt and black pepper
1 tablespoon garlic, minced
1 tablespoon Italian seasoning
¼ cup red wine vinegar
Salt and freshly ground black pepper
¼ cup green olives, finely chopped
½ cup shredded mozzarella
4 panini sandwich buns

Directions

1. Heat the grill to medium-high heat.
2. Brush the veggies with 14 cups of canola oil, season with salt and pepper, and grill until tender and slightly browned (about 3 minutes per side). Place them on a baking sheet or tray.
3. To create the dressing, combine the garlic, Italian seasoning, vinegar, 14 cups canola oil, and salt and pepper to taste in a mixing bowl.
4. Drizzle the grilled veggies with half of the dressing.
5. Toss the remaining dressing with the chopped olives.
6. Spread the olive dressing on the bottom of each panini before layering the veggies on top.
7. Sprinkle with cheese and top with remaining bread slices.
8. Grill or toast the sandwiches in a Panini press for around 5 minutes.

Hero Meatball Parmigiana

4 servings
Time to Prepare: 5 minutes
Time to cook: 23 minutes

Ingredients
2 cups Traditional Italian Sauce (store-bought or homemade)
16 1-ounce meatballs, fully-cooked, frozen
4 long submarine or hoagies rolls, split
1 cup shredded mozzarella cheese
Grated Parmesan cheese

Directions
1. Bring the meatballs and sauce to a boil, then reduce to a simmer for 3 minutes.
2. Reduce to low heat and simmer for 20 minutes, stirring regularly.
3. Divide the meatballs and sauce among the buns.
4. Garnish with mozzarella and Parmesan.

PASTA

Pasta Made From Scratch Dough yields

 6 servings.
Preparation Time: 45 minutes + 1 hour for dough resting
Time to cook: 3 minutes

Ingredients
1 pound (3 ⅓ cups) of all-purpose flour
4 whole eggs plus 1 yolk
¼ cup extra-virgin olive oil
⅛ teaspoon kosher salt
1 to 2 tablespoons water, or as if needed

Directions

1. Arrange the flour in an 8-inch-wide stack on a clean, dry work area.
2. In the middle, make a well.

3. Crack all of the eggs into a well, then add the excess yolk, olive oil, salt, and water.

4. Using a fork, combine the eggs, olive oil, water, and salt. If the edges of the well are broken, the egg mixture will flow. If you're worried about the liquid splattering all over your work area, do it in a bowl.

5. Begin incorporating the flour into the egg mixture with a fork. The dough may be lumpy.

6. Once the liquid components have been thoroughly combined and the mixture is no longer runny, begin mixing it with your hands. If the dough is dry, moisten your hands first.

7. When the mixture is uniform, start kneading on a floured surface. Wet your hands again if the dough seems too dry and stiff.

8. Use your body weight to expand the dough rather than tearing it. Knead with the heels of your hands until it is smooth and silky (about 8-15 minutes).

9. Wrap the dough in plastic wrap and set aside for at least an hour. It may be stored in the refrigerator or frozen for later use.

10. The dough should be at room temperature before shaping.

11 Roll it up and cut it into the form you choose.

12 To cook, use 6 quarts of water for 1 pound of pasta.

13. Freshly cooked pasta takes 1-3 minutes to cook.

Pasta Sauce from Scratch (Marinara)

4-6 people
Time to prepare: 20 minutes
Time to cook: 35 minutes to 2 hours

Ingredients
8 large fresh tomatoes or 12 Roma tomatoes, seeded and diced into small pieces, OR 2 cans of diced tomatoes
½ cup olive oil
8 cloves fresh garlic, minced
¾ cup fresh basil, minced OR 1 tablespoon dried basil
½ teaspoon salt
1 teaspoon fresh ground black pepper

Optional ingredients
¼ teaspoon red pepper flakes, crushed
1 teaspoon sugar
⅛ teaspoon of each marjoram and/or oregano
Parmesan cheese

Directions

1. Heat the olive oil in a large skillet or saucepan over medium heat.
2. Saute the garlic until it is soft.
3. Stir in the tomatoes and simmer until cooked through.
4. Combine the basil and the other ingredients, EXCEPT the Parmesan, in a mixing bowl. Simmer until the required thickness is reached (35 minutes for "fresher" sauce or 2 hours for thicker consistency).
5. Spoon the sauce over the cooked pasta and top with Parmesan cheese.

Gnocchi

Serves 12 people.
Time to Prepare: 35 minutes
Cooking Time: 45 minutes for the potatoes, plus 2-5 minutes for the gnocchi.

Ingredients
3 pounds russet or Idaho potatoes
2 cups all-purpose flour
1 egg, extra-large
1 pinch salt
½ cup canola oil, if needed
Pasta sauce, homemade or store-bought
Grated Parmesan

Directions

1. Boil the potatoes, unpeeled, for 45 minutes, or until tender.
2. While the potatoes are still warm (they may turn mushy as they cool), feed them through a vegetable mill or ricer onto a clean pasta board. (Alternatively, a grater may be used.)
3. Allow them to come to room temperature.

4. Make a well in the middle of the potatoes and sprinkle with the remaining flour.

5. Place the egg and salt in the middle of the well and whisk with a fork until the egg is completely integrated.

6. Flour your hands and bring the dough together.

7. Gently knead the dough until it is smooth and soft but not elastic (about 4 minutes). Put a pinch in hot water to see whether it works. If the dough does not dissolve in the water, it is ready.

8. Roll the dough into a ball and gently flatten it. Make 8 equal wedges out of it.

9. Using a wedge, layout a 12-inch diameter rope.

10. Cut the rope into 12-inch lengths. Repeat with the remaining wedges.

11. Now is the time to start preparing the water for the gnocchi. In a big saucepan, bring 6 quarts of water to a boil. Prepare 6 cups of cold water to quickly chill cooked gnocchi if you wish to keep it later.

12. In the meanwhile, form the gnocchi by rolling a portion of the sliced dough along the backside of the tines of a fork. Cover with a cloth and place them on a floured tray. These may be frozen and wrapped in plastic wrap for later use.

13. To cook, place these pieces (if frozen, do not defrost) in a pot of boiling water and simmer, stirring gently until they float (approximately 1 minute). Cook in batches and don't overcrowd the pan.

14. Remove the gnocchi using a slotted spoon or spider sieve and place it on a serving plate.

15. At this time, chill the cooked gnocchi in cold water, then drain and stir with 12 cups of canola oil. Store it in the refrigerator, covered, for up to 48 hours.

16. To serve fresh, cooked gnocchi, drizzle with warm sauce and top with grated Parmesan.

Meat Sauce on Spaghetti (Bolognese)

10 servings
Time to Prepare: 5 minutes
Time to cook: 35 minutes

Ingredients
2 (24 ounce) jars Marinara sauce or 3 cups homemade pasta sauce
1 (16 ounces) can crushed tomatoes
1 onion, chopped
2 tablespoons olive oil
1 pound of ground beef
1 pound Italian sausage, casings removed
½ cup pepperoni, finely chopped
1 teaspoon Italian seasonings or a combination of basil, oregano, rosemary, and thyme to taste
¼ cup red wine (preferably Chianti or Sangiovese)
10 ounces spaghetti noodles, cooked according to the packaging instructions

Directions

1. Heat the olive oil and onions in a large saucepan over medium-high heat. Cook, stirring occasionally until the onions are transparent.
2. Stir in the marina sauce and crushed tomatoes, then reduce to low heat.
3. Meanwhile, cook the ground beef and Italian sausage in a pan until well done.
4. Remove any extra fat from the meat and place it in the saucepan with the sauce.
5. Combine the chopped pepperoni, Italian spices, and red wine in a mixing bowl.
6. Simmer for approximately 20 minutes, seasoning with salt and pepper as needed.
7. Ladle the sauce over the cooked spaghetti noodles. If preferred, top with grated Parmesan.

Meatballs on Spaghetti

6-8 people
Time to Prepare: 15 minutes
Time to cook: 45 minutes

Ingredients
2 (30 ounces) jars of spaghetti sauce or 3 ¾ cups of homemade pasta sauce
1 pound spaghetti, cooked al dente

For meatballs
2 pounds lean ground beef
2 eggs
¾ cup dry bread crumbs
¼ cup fresh parsley, chopped
2 garlic cloves, minced
½ teaspoon salt or to taste
¼ cup Parmesan cheese

Directions

1. In a mixing dish, thoroughly combine all of the meatball ingredients.
2. Form the meatball mixture into 18 meatballs.
3. Bring the sauce to a simmer in a saucepan.
4. Return to a simmer and add the meatballs.
5. Cook, covered, for 35-40 minutes, or until the meatballs are cooked through.
6. Toss the sauce and meatballs with the heated noodles.

Alfredo Fettuccine

Serves: 2-3
Preparation Time: 5 minutes
Cooking Time: 15 minutes

Ingredients
1 (8 ounces) package fettuccine, cooked according to packaging instructions and drained
¼ cup water, reserved for cooking pasta
3 tablespoons unsalted butter
1 small shallot, finely minced
½ cup heavy cream
¾ cup freshly Parmigiano-Reggiano or Parmesan, grated
¼ teaspoon salt
Freshly ground black pepper, to taste

Fresh basil
Parmigiano-Reggiano or Parmesan, grated

Directions

1. In a large frying pan or heavy-bottomed pot, melt the butter over medium-high heat.
2. Cook the shallots until they are tender (about 2 minutes).
3. Bring the cream to a low boil.
4. Reduce the heat to medium-low and continue to cook for 3 minutes.
5. Remove from the heat and whisk in the cheese, salt, and pepper until smooth.
6. Stir in the cooked pasta and saved pasta water.
7. Return the pan to the burner over medium-high heat and gently mix in the pasta to coat it with the sauce.
8. Serve garnished with Parmigiano-Reggiano and fresh basil.

Traditional Lasagna

10 servings
Time to prepare: 1 hour 35 minutes
Time to cook: 30 minutes

Ingredients
16 flat "no-boil" lasagna noodles
4 cups mozzarella cheese, grated, divided

For meat sauce
1 large yellow onion, chopped
1 tablespoon olive oil
2 cloves garlic, peeled and minced
1 pound ground beef, preferably sirloin
1 pound ground Italian sausage
1 teaspoon kosher salt
1 tablespoon dried basil
1 tablespoon dried oregano
1 tablespoon dried parsley
12 ounces tomato paste
1 (28 ounces) can whole San Marzano tomatoes
¼ cup red wine or water

For cheese sauce
3 cups whole milk ricotta
2 eggs
2 tablespoons fresh parsley, chopped
½ teaspoon freshly ground black pepper
½ cup Parmesan cheese, freshly grated

Meat Sauce Preparation Instructions
1. In a medium-sized saucepan, sauté the onion in olive oil over medium heat.
2. Cook, stirring constantly, until the garlic, meat, and sausage are browned.
3. Combine the salt, basil, parsley, and oregano in a mixing bowl.
4. Add the tomato paste and mix well.
5. Remove the San Marzano tomatoes one at a time, smashing each one with your palm over the sauce to gather the liquid. Combine the smashed tomato with the sauce.
6. Swirl the can of wine or water to extract any residual tomato juice and pour it into the saucepan. Reduce the heat to low and stir.
7. Simmer for 45 minutes, covered.

To make the cheese sauce
8. Combine ricotta, eggs, parsley, black pepper, and Parmesan in a large mixing basin.
9. Store in the refrigerator until ready to construct the lasagna.

To make the lasagna
10. Preheat the oven to 375°F and butter a 13x9 baking pan with cooking spray.
11. Cover the bottom of the baking pan with 1 cup of beef sauce.
12 Layer 4 lasagna noodles on top of the meat sauce.
13 Spread 13 cups of the cheese sauce on top, then sprinkle with 12 cups of mozzarella.
14. Continue stacking until the meat sauce is topped with mozzarella.
15. Bake the lasagna for 30-40 minutes, or until the cheese is brown. Allow for a 10-minute rest before serving.

Creamy Pesto Linguini

6 servings
Time to Prepare: 10 minutes
Time to cook: 3 minutes

Ingredients
⅓ cup extra-virgin olive oil
½ cup heavy cream
2 tablespoons butter
1 (12 ounces) pack linguine pasta, cooked according to packaging instructions and drained

Pesto Sauce
¾ cup fresh basil leaves
¾ cup grated Parmesan cheese, divided
3 tablespoons pine nuts
2 cloves garlic, peeled
½ teaspoon kosher salt
½ teaspoon freshly ground pepper

Directions

1. In a food processor, mix the basil, 12 cups Parmesan cheese, pine nuts, garlic, salt, and pepper to create the pesto.
To blend, pulse many times.
2. While processing, drip in the oil gently.
3. Melt the butter and cream together in a skillet over medium heat.
4. Stir in the pesto and continue to cook for 3 minutes.
5. Remove from the fire and mix in the remaining Parmesan.
6. Finally, add the drained linguine and well combine.

Carbonara Fettuccini

Preparation Time: 10 minutes
Servings: 6
Time to cook: 25 minutes

Ingredients
1 tablespoon olive oil
4 shallots, peeled and diced
1 large onion, peeled and sliced
1 pound bacon, cut into strips
1 clove of garlic, chopped
1 (16 ounces) packet fettuccine, cooked according to packaging instructions
3 egg yolks
½ cup cream
¾ cup Parmesan cheese, shredded
Salt and pepper to taste

Directions

1. Place the fettuccine in a serving dish or bowl and drain it. Set it aside for now.
2. Heat the olive oil in a large saucepan over medium heat and sauté the shallots until tender.
3. Stir in the onion and bacon.
4. When the bacon is just starting to brown, add the garlic and remove it from the fire.
5. In the meanwhile, whisk together the eggs, cream, and Parmesan in a mixing dish.
6. Ladle the bacon mixture over the spaghetti.
7. Stir in the cream mixture, salt, and pepper.

Linguini with Seafood (Linguini al Frutti di Mare)

Serves 4 Time to Prepare:
15 minutes
Time to cook: 15 minutes

Ingredients
2 ¼ pounds mixed shellfish (like clams, mussels, scampi, unpeeled shrimp or prawns), cleaned
¼ cup dry white wine
25-30 cherry tomatoes, halved, seeded, and juiced
1 (16 ounces) pack dried linguine, cooked according to packaging directions, drained
½ cup olive oil
5 garlic cloves, thinly sliced
⅛ teaspoon dried chili flakes, or to taste
3 tablespoons flat-leaf parsley, chopped
Salt and freshly ground black pepper, to taste

Directions
1. Begin with the mussels and clams. After washing, combine them with the wine in a saucepan.
2. Cook, covered, over high heat until the shells open (about 4 minutes). Remove and discard any unopened shellfish.
Set aside the clams and mussels that have been opened. All except roughly 2 tablespoons of the cooking liquid should be saved.
3. Chop the cherry tomatoes, which have been seeded and pressed.
4. Meanwhile, heat the olive oil and garlic in a large skillet over low heat until the garlic starts to crackle.
5. Simmer for 5 minutes after adding the chili flakes and diced tomatoes.
6. Return the clams' strained, saved liquid to the pot and bring it back to a boil.
7. Simmer until the liquid has been reduced by half.
8. Place the scampi in the sauce and cook until pink, turning once.
9. Add the prawns and cook until done (about 3 minutes).

10. Add the cooked clams and mussels and mix well.
11. Stir in the parsley and simmer, stirring regularly, until the seafood is cooked through.
12. If preferred, season with salt and pepper.
13. Pour over cooked pasta and toss to coat.

Spicy Shrimp in a Creamy Sauce (Fra Diavolo)

4 servings
Time to Prepare: 15 minutes
Time to cook: 18 minutes

Ingredients
1 pound large shrimp, peeled and deveined
1 teaspoon salt, or as needed
1 teaspoon dried crushed red pepper flakes
4-5 tablespoons olive oil, divided
1 medium onion, sliced
1 (14 ½ ounce) can of diced tomatoes, juice retained
1 cup dry white wine
3 cloves garlic, chopped
¼ teaspoon dried oregano leaves
3 tablespoon fresh Italian parsley leaves, chopped
3 tablespoon fresh basil leaves, chopped
Cooked pasta for serving

Directions
1. Combine the shrimp, salt, and red pepper flakes in a mixing dish.
2. In a large skillet over medium-high heat, heat 3 tablespoons of oil.

3. Add the shrimp and heat until they are barely cooked through (approximately 2 minutes). Put it in a bowl and put it aside.
4. Sauté the onion in 1 to 2 tablespoons olive oil in the same pan until transparent (about 5 minutes).
5. Combine the undrained tomatoes, wine, garlic, and oregano in a mixing bowl.
6. Simmer until the sauce thickens (about 10 minutes)
7. Add the shrimp and their juices back to the tomato mixture.
8. Toss and cook for 1 minute more.
9. Stir in the parsley, basil, and salt to taste. Serve with spaghetti.

Pasta with Veggies (Primavera)

Preparation Time: 25 minutes
 Servings: 6
Time to cook: 20 minutes

Ingredients
3 carrots, peeled and julienned
2 medium zucchini or 1 large zucchini, julienned
2 yellow squash, julienned
1 onion, thinly sliced
1 yellow bell pepper, julienned
1 red bell pepper, julienned
¼ cup olive oil
Kosher salt and freshly ground black pepper
1 tablespoon dried Italian herbs
1 pound farfalle (bowtie pasta), cooked according to packaging instructions
15 cherry tomatoes, halved
½ cup grated Parmesan

Directions

1. Preheat the oven to 450 degrees Fahrenheit.
2. Toss the veggies in a large mixing bowl with the oil, salt, pepper, and dry herbs to coat.
3. Arrange the veggies in a single layer on two baking sheets.
Do not overcrowd.
4. Bake for approximately 20 minutes, tossing and turning halfway through, until the veggies start to brown.
5. Drain the trays and set aside approximately 1 cup of the veggie juice.
6. Combine the pasta, roasted veggies, cherry tomatoes, and saved liquid in a large mixing bowl.
7. Season with salt and pepper to taste.
8. Garnish with Parmesan and serve.

Pasta tossed with capers, olives, and tomatoes (Puttanesca)

4 servings
Time to Prepare: 10 minutes
Time to cook: 25 minutes

Ingredients
1 (14 ounces) package spaghetti, cooked according to packaging instructions, drained
2 tablespoons olive oil
2 cloves garlic, chopped
1 small red chili, finely chopped
1 cup pitted black olives, sliced
6 sundried tomatoes, cut into thin strips
2 anchovy fillets, chopped (optional)
2 tablespoons salted capers, rinsed
1 (14 ½ ounce) can of diced tomatoes
½ cup fresh basil leaves, shredded
Grated Parmesan, to serve

Directions

1. In a pan over medium heat, heat the olive oil and sauté the garlic and chiles for 1 minute.
2. Cook for 20 minutes after adding the olives, sundried tomatoes, capers, anchovies, and diced tomatoes. Season with pepper to taste.
3. Stir in the spaghetti and season with basil.
4. Combine well.
5. Garnish with Parmesan cheese and serve.

PIZZA

Dough for Pizza

2 medium to large crusts
(serves 2)

Time to prepare: 2 hours and 10 minutes
Time to cook: 6-8 minutes (pre-baking)

Ingredients
1 tablespoon sugar
1 ⅓ cup warm water (105°F)
1 (¼ ounce) packet of active dry yeast (2 ¼ teaspoons)
3 tablespoons extra-virgin olive oil, plus more for brushing
3 ¾ cups all-purpose flour, plus more for dusting
1 ½ teaspoons salt

Directions

1. Dissolve the sugar in warm water, then stir in the yeast. Allow it to stand until the water gets foamy (about 10 minutes). Add the olive oil and mix well.
2. Combine the flour and salt in a large mixing dish.
3. Make a well in the middle of the mixture and pour in the yeast mixture.
4. Stir with a wooden spoon until a rough dough forms.
5. Knead the dough on a floured surface until it is smooth and elastic (about 5 minutes).
6. Lightly coat two bowls with olive oil.
7. Cut the dough in half as evenly as possible (about 1 pound each piece).
8. Brush the surface of each part of the dough with oil before placing it in a prepared bowl.
9. Wrap the dough in plastic wrap and allow it to double in size (about 1 hour and 30 minutes).
Roll out into the appropriate shape and diameter. The dough may be wrapped in plastic wrap and frozen for up to a month.
11. If using a pre-baked crust, bake at 425°F until lightly browned (about 6-8 minutes)

Pizza Sauce from Scratch

2-4 people
Preparation 15-minute time limit
1 hour and 10 minutes of cooking time

Ingredients
1 (28 ounces) can whole peeled tomatoes
1 tablespoon extra-virgin olive oil
1 tablespoon unsalted butter
2 medium cloves garlic, grated
2 anchovy fillets (optional)
1 teaspoon dried oregano
Pinch red pepper flakes
⅛ teaspoon kosher salt, or to taste
2 sprigs of fresh basil, leaves attached
1 medium yellow onion, peeled and halved
1 teaspoon sugar
⅛ cup red wine (optional)

Directions

1. Using a blender, food processor, or food mill, puree the tomatoes into a chunky (not smooth) consistency. Place aside.
2. Melt the butter and oil in a saucepan over low to medium heat.
3. Add the garlic, anchovies (optional), oregano, pepper flakes, and salt after the butter has melted. When sautéing anchovies, crush them with a wooden spoon or a fork.
4. Cook, stirring constantly until the garlic is slightly caramelized (approximately 3- 4 minutes).
5. Combine the chopped tomatoes, basil, onion, sugar, and red wine in a mixing bowl (optional).
6. Simmer over very low heat, stirring periodically, until reduced by 12 (about 1 hour).
7. Cut the onion and basil stems from the stems.
8. Taste and adjust the seasoning with salt or more pepper flakes as desired.
9. Remove from the oven and set aside to cool to room temperature.
10. Store in the refrigerator for up to 2 weeks.

Cheese pizza

8 servings
Preparation time: 5 minutes + 45 minutes in the freezer
Time to cook: 10-12 minutes

Ingredients :

1 (12 inches) round of pizza dough
¼ -⅓ cup pizza sauce or all-purpose tomato sauce
2 cups mozzarella cheese, shredded and then frozen
1 tablespoon fresh basil, chopped finely

Directions

1. Preheat the oven to 450 degrees Fahrenheit for 45 minutes to an hour before baking.
2. Freeze the shredded mozzarella for at least 20 minutes.
3. Place the pizza dough on a lightly oiled baking sheet or pizza stone.
4. Spread the sauce outward from the center of the dough, leaving approximately a half-inch border around the outside.
5. Evenly sprinkle with shredded mozzarella and basil.

6. Bake for 10-12 minutes, or until the crust is set and the cheese bubbles.
7. Best when served hot.

Hawaiian Pizza

Serves 8-12 people.
Time to Prepare: 10 minutes
Time to cook: 21 minutes

Ingredients
1 (15 inches) round of pizza dough
1 ¾ cups pizza sauce
2 cups shredded mozzarella cheese, divided
1 cup shredded Romano cheese, divided
1 ½ cup cooked ham, diced
1 cup pineapple tidbits, drained

Directions

1. Preheat the oven to 425°F and coat a 15-inch pizza pan with cooking spray.
2. Press the dough into the pan, gently raising the sides.
3. Bake until the top is gently browned (about 6-8 minutes).
4. Spread the sauce outward in a circular motion, starting from the middle of the crust and leaving half an inch around the edge.
5. Top with 1 34 cup mozzarella and 12 cups Romano cheese.

6. Arrange the ham and pineapple on top, followed by the remaining cheese.

7. Bake until the cheese has melted and the crust has become golden brown (about 15 minutes)

Super Meat Pizza

Serves 8 people.
Time to Prepare: 25 minutes
Time to cook: 15 minutes

Ingredients
Pizza dough rolled out to make a 15-inch crust or 15- by 10-inch
Rectangular crust
½ pound lean ground beef
½ pound Italian sausage, casing removed
½ cup pizza sauce
½ cup sliced pepperoni
1 ounce thinly sliced salami, cut into quarters
½ cup prosciutto or bacon, diced
1 cup cheddar cheese, shredded
1 cup mozzarella cheese, shredded

Directions

1. Preheat the oven to 400 degrees Fahrenheit.
2. Grease a pizza pan with olive oil. Fit the dough into the pan.
3. Cook the meat and sausage in a nonstick frying pan over

medium-high heat, stirring constantly. The meat should be thoroughly done and the sausage should be no longer pink (about 6 to 8 minutes). Remove from the pan and place on paper towels to drain.

4. Spread the pizza sauce to within a half-inch of the dough's edges.
5. Stir in the drained ground meat and sausage.
6. Arrange the remaining ingredients on top of the pizza.
7. Bake for 15 minutes, or until the crust is golden brown and the cheese has melted (13 to 16 minutes).

Pizza with Pepperoni

Serves 8 people.
Time to prepare: 2 hours and 20 minutes
Time to cook: 15 minutes

Ingredients
Pizza dough rolled into a 13-inch diameter crust
1 tablespoon olive oil
½ cup pizza sauce
2 cups mozzarella cheese, grated
¼ cup Parmesan cheese, finely grated
30 slices of Italian pepperoni
⅛ teaspoon crushed red pepper flakes
Fresh basil leaves for garnish

Directions
1. Preheat the oven to 450 degrees Fahrenheit.
2. Place the pizza dough on a prepared baking sheet.
3. Drizzle olive oil over the whole surface of the pizza dough.
4. Spread pizza sauce evenly over the dough, leaving approximately a half-inch border around the borders for the crust.
5. Evenly distribute the Parmesan and mozzarella over the sauce.
6. Arrange the Italian pepperoni on top of the pizza.
7. Bake for 15 minutes, or until the crust is golden brown and the cheese has melted (about 12-15 minutes).
8. Allow it cool for approximately 10 minutes before sprinkling with basil leaves.

Pesto Veggie Pizza

Serves 6 people.
Time to Prepare: 25 minutes
Time to cook: 10 minutes

Ingredients
1 prebaked 12-inch thin pizza crust dough
2 cups fresh mushrooms, sliced
1 cup fresh broccoli florets, chopped
¾ cup zucchini, thinly sliced
½ cup sweet yellow pepper, julienned
½ cup sweet red pepper, julienned
1 small red onion, thinly sliced and separated into rings
1-2 tablespoons pesto sauce
½ cup pizza sauce or all-purpose tomato sauce
¼ cup grated Romano or Parmesan cheese
¼ cup ripe olives, sliced
¾ cup shredded mozzarella cheese

Directions

1. Preheat the oven to 450 degrees Fahrenheit.
2. In a pizza pan or on a pizza stone, place a pre-baked crust.

3. Meanwhile, heat a skillet over medium heat with nonstick frying spray or vegetable oil.

4. Cook the mushrooms, broccoli, zucchini, peppers, and onion in a skillet until soft.

5. Take the pan off the heat and whisk in the pesto. Set aside the pan.

Spread the pizza sauce on top of the pizza dough.

7. Arrange the sautéed veggies and olives on a platter and top with the cheeses.

8. Bake for 20 minutes, or until the crust is golden brown and the cheese has melted (about 10-12 minutes).

Pizza Bianca (White Pizza) with Chicken and Broccoli

15 people
Time to Prepare: 15 minutes
Time to cook: 20 minutes

Ingredients
1 recipe for pizza dough
1 tablespoon dried parsley flakes
1 tablespoon dried chopped onion
2 skinless chicken breasts, pre-grilled or sautéed, cubed
1 (13 ounces) pack frozen broccoli florets, thawed
4 cups shredded mozzarella cheese, divided
3 tablespoons Parmesan cheese, or as desired

Directions
1. Preheat the oven to 450 degrees Fahrenheit.
2. Pat and stretch the pizza dough to fit a cookie sheet that has been gently oiled.
3. Scatter chopped onion and parsley flakes over the dough.
4. Bake for 5 minutes on the bottom rack.
5. Remove the pan from the oven and set aside for 10 minutes before topping with 3 cups of mozzarella.

6. Stir in the broccoli and chicken.
7. In the meanwhile, lower the oven temperature to 350°F.
8. Sprinkle the leftover mozzarella cheese on top of the pizza.
9. Bake the pizza on the center rack for 10 minutes to cook the ingredients and melt the cheese (about 15 minutes).
10. Garnish with Parmesan and serve.

Pizza with Spicy Sausage and Mushrooms from Italy

Serves 6

Preparation Time: 10 minutes + 15 minutes for dough resting

Time to cook: 25-30 minutes

Ingredients

1 pound refrigerated ready-made or homemade pizza dough

Cooking spray

6 ounces spicy Italian sausage (1 large sausage)

1 cup onion, thinly sliced

1 (8 ounces) package mushrooms, sliced

1 cup red or green bell pepper, seeded and diced

1 tablespoon yellow cornmeal, or more, for dusting

½ cup pizza sauce or all-purpose tomato sauce

½ cup shredded mozzarella cheese

¼ cup grated Parmigiano-Reggiano cheese

Directions

1. Allow the chilled dough to rest for 15 minutes.
2. Preheat the oven to 450 degrees Fahrenheit.

3. Remove the sausage from its casing and sauté it in a nonstick pan until crumbly (about 3 minutes). As it cooks, break it up with a spatula.
4. Add the onions and mushrooms and sauté for 4 minutes, or until tender.
5. Saute the bell pepper until aromatic (about 3 minutes).
6. Cornmeal the work surface.
7. Gently pat and stretch the dough before placing it on the dusted surface.
8. Press it down and spread it with your hands, then roll it out to create a 12-inch circle using a dusted rolling pin.
9. Spread the dough out on the pizza pan, stretching and shaping it as required with your hands.
10. Spoon the pizza sauce into the middle of the dough and spread it out to the edges, leaving approximately a half-inch border free of sauce.
11 Spread the sausage and veggie combination on top.
12. Sprinkle with mozzarella and then Parmesan.
13. Bake for 15-20 minutes, or until the cheese is golden brown and bubbling.

1 pound chilled ready-made pizza dough or handmade pizza dough
Spray cooking oil
6 oz. hot Italian sausage (1 large sausage)
1 cup finely sliced onion
1 (8 ounces) box sliced mushrooms 1 cup seeded and chopped red or green bell pepper
1 tablespoon yellow cornmeal, plus more if desired, for dusting
12 cup pizza sauce or tomato sauce (all-purpose)
12 cup shredded mozzarella
14 cup grated Parmigiano-Reggiano

Pizza with BBQ Chicken

6-8 people
Time to Prepare: 5 minutes
Time to cook: 8-12 minutes

Ingredients
1 (12 inches) pre-baked pizza crust
¼ cup pizza sauce
¼ cup barbecue sauce
1 cup cooked chicken, shredded
2 cups Italian 5 cheese blend, shredded
8 garlic cloves, roasted
1 red onion, sliced
Italian parsley, for garnish

Directions
1. Preheat the oven to 450 degrees Fahrenheit.
2. Arrange the pre-baked crust on a pizza pan or stone.
3. Combine the pizza and barbecue sauce in a mixing bowl, then distribute it over the crust.
4. Top with 1 cup of cheese.

5. Combine the chicken, garlic, and onion in a mixing bowl.
6. Sprinkle with the remaining cheese.
7. Bake the pizza for 8-12 minutes, or until the cheese is melted and bubbling. Garnish with parsley.
8. Slice and serve

CHICKEN

Parmigiana chicken

4 servings
Time to Prepare: 30 minutes
Time to cook: 45 minutes

Ingredients
4 pieces of boneless skinless chicken breast, pounded thin
Salt and pepper
1 large egg, beaten with ½ tablespoon water
½ cup all-purpose flour
1 cup panko bread crumbs
¼ cup vegetable oil
All-Purpose Tomato Sauce, recipe below
1 pound fresh mozzarella, thinly sliced
¼ cup freshly grated Parmesan
Sliced green onion, for garnish
Fettuccini with tomato sauce for serving

All-Purpose Tomato Sauce

2 tablespoons olive oil
1 large onion, finely chopped
4 cloves garlic, smashed to a paste with a pinch of salt
2 (28 ounce) can plum tomatoes, undrained, pureed in a blender
1 (16 ounces) can crushed tomatoes
1 (2 ½ ounce) can of tomato paste
1 bay leaf
½ cup Italian parsley
1 small yellow bell pepper, chopped
Salt and freshly ground pepper

Sauce preparation instructions

1. Heat the olive oil in a saucepan over medium heat.
2. Saute the onions and garlic until tender.
3. Bring the pureed tomatoes and liquids, crushed tomatoes, tomato paste, bay leaf, parsley, and bell pepper to a boil. Season with salt and pepper to taste.
4. Reduce the heat to low and simmer for 30 minutes, or until slightly thickened.
5. Allow to cool to room temperature before storing in jars in the refrigerator.

Regarding the chicken

Preheat the oven to 400 degrees Fahrenheit.
7. Season the chicken well with salt and pepper.
8. Lightly coat with flour and tap to remove any excess.
9. Dip the bread in the egg mixture, allowing any excess to fall off.
10. Evenly coat with bread crumbs.
11. Heat the oil in a pan on the stovetop until it is nearly smoking.
12. Brown both sides of the breasts (approximately 30-40 seconds on each side).
13 Place the chicken on a baking sheet.
14. Place 1-2 tablespoons of tomato sauce, slices of mozzarella, and roughly 1 tablespoon of Parmesan on top of each chicken piece.
15. Season with salt and pepper to taste.

16. Bake until the chicken is well cooked and the cheese has melted (about 5 to 7 minutes).
17. Garnish with green onion and serve over spaghetti, if preferred, with tomato sauce.

DESSERT (DOLCI)

Tiramisu

Serves: 2
Preparation Time: 15 minutes plus 2 hours refrigeration
Cooking Time: 0 minutes

Ingredients
4 pieces of ladyfinger biscuit
¼ teaspoon cocoa powder for dusting

Mascarpone Mixture
1 egg yolk, should be very fresh, preferably free-range
2 tablespoons sugar
1 teaspoon vanilla essence
1 cup mascarpone
2 teaspoons milk, or as needed

Espresso Dip
1 cup espresso, warm
1 tablespoon Kahlua (optional)
1 tablespoon sugar

Directions

Mascarpone Concoction
1. Whisk together the yolk, sugar, and vanilla extract until thoroughly combined, then fold in the mascarpone.
2. If the mascarpone is too hard, add the milk gradually to soften it.
3. Whisk until smooth.

4. Combine the ingredients in a mixing bowl and whisk until the sugar is fully dissolved.

To make the Tiramisu
5. Make two dessert dishes or cups.
6. Soak a ladyfinger in espresso for a few minutes before cutting it in half. As the initial layer, place it in the bowl/cup.
7. Top with roughly a quarter of the mascarpone mixture.
8. For the third layer, soak and break another lady's finger.
9. Add another layer of mascarpone and sift with cocoa powder using a sieve over the dessert cup.
10th. Repeat with the second dessert dish.
11. Refrigerate for 2 hours before serving.

Cannoli (homemade)

Serves 12-25 people.
Time to prepare: 20 minutes + 2 hours refrigerating
Time to cook: 10-15 minutes

Ingredients
Egg white, for sealing
Oil for frying, 3 inches deep

Cannoli shell
2 ⅓ cups flour
1 ½ tablespoons sugar
2 tablespoons butter
1 egg
⅛ teaspoon salt
¾ cup Marsala dry wine

Cream Filling
2 cups ricotta cheese
2 cups confectioner's sugar, sifted
2 tablespoons rum
¼ teaspoon vanilla extract

3 ounces bitter chocolate, broken into tiny chips
Directions

To create the shells,
1. In a large mixing bowl, combine the shell ingredients to produce a smooth, somewhat sticky dough.
2. Wrap the dough in plastic wrap and place it in the refrigerator for 2 hours or overnight.
3. Divide the dough into two equal halves. While you work, keep the leftover dough covered and cold.
4. Flour a work area lightly and lay out the dough to approximately 18 inches thick.
5. Cut out 3 to 5-inch diameter circles.
6. Form an oval out of each cut-out circle.
7. Brush the outsides of the cannoli tubes with olive oil. Cannelloni pasta may also be used as tubes.
8. Wrap the ovals around each tube and dab a little egg white on the edges where they overlap. To seal, press firmly. Allow them to rest for the egg white to set.
9. Heat the oil in a large saucepan or electric deep-fryer to 375°F, or until a small piece of dough sizzles and browns in 1 minute.
10. Fry the shells until golden, approximately 2 minutes (turning halfway through).
11. Use a wire skimmer or a big slotted spoon to lift. To let the oil flow back into the pan, grip the cannoli vertically over the fryer with tongs.
12. Pat dry with paper towels. Rep with the rest of the tubes.
13. Using a potholder, grip the tubes and peel the cannoli shells off with tongs while they are still hot.
14. Allow cooling fully on paper towels.

To make the filling
15. Using a wire whisk, cream the ricotta in a large mixing dish.
16. Combine the remaining ingredients in a large mixing bowl and well combine.
17. Fill a pastry tube with the filling and pipe it into the shells.
18. Finish with a dusting of confectioner's sugar and serve.

Conclusion

Italian-American cuisine has been so ingrained in American culinary culture that it is now regarded as really American. It's no surprise that Americans have embraced Italian-inspired cuisine. Though it has evolved through time as Italian immigrants have adapted to American society, the spirit and passion of traditional Italian food persist. Italian cuisine will always be comfort food, and this cookbook allows us to bring that warmth into our own homes.

Good appetite!

9 7 8 3 9 8 6 5 3 7 7 9 1